MENDING

THE

WHEEL

By

ELLEN
J
GOULDSBROUGH

Published in Wales by

Golden Eagle Publishing
PO Box 10
Llandrindod Wells
LD1 5WJ
POWYS
WALES

Printed by
Antony Rowe
Eastbourne
East Sussex

ISBN: 1-902043-10-3

FOREWORD

———◆———

"Mending The Wheel" is a joint venture between myself and the world of Spirit, with the vast majority of the work undertaken by the latter.

It has been written with all in mind, whether newly awoken, long awake, or merely stirring in the space between wakefulness and sleep.

It is a work that is hoped will, upon each reading, produce more and more food for deep thought, as well as answering, perhaps, a few questions as we are encouraged to step outside our personal boundaries and see what we have blinded ourselves to. To begin to see what we can do to improve Earth's situation, therefore, and our own, as well as help to improve circumstances elsewhere in the universe.

Perhaps, most importantly, it also teaches us that no man, woman or child is an island, for we all belong to one enormous family - the family of creation - no matter how far and wide that creation spreads. Because of this one simple fact, we all have responsibilities not only to ourselves but to the WHOLE family whether we like it or not!

ACKNOWLEDGEMENT

———————◆———————

For the cover design of this book and for the unsigned poetry amongst its pages I thank Darren, my younger son.

For lending me their ears during the writing of it I thank both my sons, Darren and Paul.

Ellen J Gouldsbrough

———————◆———————

CONTENTS

Today	1
Introduction - The Hub	2
My Light	5
1—Inner Wheel (I)	6
Can You?	14
Inner Wheel (II)	15
A Blade Of Grass	21
2—Middle Wheel	22
Soul Song	33
3—Outer Wheel (I)	34
The Invitation	42
Outer Wheel (II)	43
My Gift To You	51

TODAY

Anything good in the paper you say.
Not likely, it shows the state of the world today.
It's all there in black and white,
In plain view but out of sight,
You read of kids slaughtered at an early age,
Ignore the blood and turn the page.
You see pictures of forests being burned,
Stare amazed at the colour snaps, 'til another page is
turned.
Onto the cartoons, have a grin,
Forget the people caught in war or just starving and thin.
Read your stars, what have they got to say?
Bet they didn't tell her she'd be raped and killed today.
Few more pages give 'em a quick look,
Just a mugging and robbery, nothing with that sensational
hook
To keep you glued to the page.
Miss the story about the pitiful animal in the tiny cage,
Now the sport, what's happening here?
Oh God no, United lost, wipe away a quick tear.
England have lost once again,
Feel nothing for murderers but hate those eleven men.
In today's society race and colour don't matter at all,
Tell that to the Asians and Blacks beaten on their way to
school.
One more copper is killed, he won't see today's Sun,
Won't read of the ten killed by a madman's gun.
At the end of the paper throw it away,
Forget what you've read, it'll be back another day.
Maybe give page three another stare,
Perhaps the front page Pamela Anderson's on there.
Nothing to do but make a cup of tea,
Pour some half fat milk on your low cal. museli.
Got to keep healthy, wouldn't do to die.
Not like the addicts outside getting high.
Put on your blinkers, make sure they're secure,
Just so you don't notice the world outside your door.
Step into the street become just another face,
Don't fear the reaper, he's all over the place.

INTRODUCTION:
THE HUB

W HAT is the universe in relation to you, other than your existence within it? What do you perceive your role in the universe to be? If indeed you feel you have one.

The universe itself vibrates on different levels. These are all inter-linked and interlaced so thoroughly that they form a mesh in which the planets, suns, moons and stars of the galaxy are held. The galaxies themselves whether known or unknown to humankind, are also held in harmonious balance within this mesh. It is necessary that they are held there, else the universe would become a celestial billiard table.

Just as there are many different forms of life on Earth, so there are throughout the universe. All are at different stages of evolution and vibrational levels, but all are a part of the same universe so all are a part of the whole. This must indicate that if all life forms are a part of the same whole and are all members of the same universal family, then each one has a role to play within that family.

All souls must take responsibility for the wellbeing of their fellow family members, as well as for the living and breathing world which is their home. Every soul must do their share of the housework.

At the moment we must be more concerned with those of us who reside upon Earth, so we will regard her as the centre or hub of the wheel.

Since the hub is too weak to support the wheel correctly the wheel we have is unsound. Earth as the hub must be made stronger to support the rest of the universe which forms the remainder of the wheel. At the moment people are beginning to realise that Earth is in dire need of help, due to the amount of greed and negativity, because of the atrocities committed upon her and to her and through neglect and selfishness. Through her gifts being taken for granted, Mother Earth's vibrations are too low to enable the wheel to turn as freely as it should. So because of the poor condition that Earth finds herself in, through no fault of her own, the other planets of the universe suffer also. Therefore all other life forms throughout the universe are suffering as well. They find themselves being unable to evolve as well as they should.

If you wondered whether or not you have a role to play within the universe, you may rest assured that you have. There is no living thing that has not.

The first step to ensuring the free movement of the wheel is in the acceptance that each soul is a being of the whole universe, and not of Earth alone, and due to this fact each has a responsibility.

Instead of narrow thinking, expand your thought processes to take in the whole. Consider a grain of sand upon a beach. How, when you move it, does the surrounding beach react? Are you able to remove a single grain without other grains moving? Try, and see. You will find that you cannot. Think of a pebble thrown by you into an expanse of water. When cast, a pebble as we all know, creates ripples that can be seen as they flow outward. But what happened beneath the water as the pebble sank beneath the surface? Did it stir up silt that clouded the water for a while affecting the life forms within? You do not know. You could not see. You were only able to see the ripples on the surface that were large enough for your eye to see. Human eyes are not capable of seeing the infinitesimal ripples, nor how far they outwardly extend. Or what happened beneath the water as a result.

Why was the pebble thrown anyway? Was it in anger, frustration, just for something to do, or was it thrown for a perfectly valid reason? Whatever the reason for the action there was a re-action, both seen and unseen.

For any action or inaction that each life form takes there is a re-action somewhere. So it is important that you consider before you act, what the effect of your action will be, not only upon yourself and those close to you, but upon all the souls with whom you are inter-dependent. Life forms whom you may never meet, but who exist. What effect will your action or inaction have upon Earth and therefore the rest of the planets in the universe?

It does not take wealth, nor mean that ritual must be observed, it only means that contemplation and/or meditation should take place so that you are able to tune into yourself. In doing this you will come to know your own individual worth as a universal being. You will also be able to acknowledge that the Great Spirit is a part of you and therefore you are a part of the Great Spirit.

The Great Spirit is the creator of the whole, so therefore is the whole, and as you carry within yourself a part of the Great Spirit then you are a part of that which was created, and therefore are responsible to it.

When you question your actions and the motives behind them, and consider the consequences of your actions before taking them, you can rest assured, that as long as you act with the right intentions your actions will have good re-actions, for yourself, your fellow beings, your planet and your universe. In this way the hub will begin to be fortified in readiness to properly be able to support the remainder of the wheel, so that it may move more freely, with the energies flowing, as they should. Unhindered and at their many different vibrations.

MY LIGHT

Deep within me a candle glows,
The light to show the way,
Just like the tide, it ebbs and flows,
Growing stronger by the day.

I try my best to fan it bright,
To live in the way that is true,
You may shun me as is your right,
But my light still shines for you.

The love of light is the light of love,
Spreading rays to all around,
They soar up high on the wings of a dove,
And gently caress the ground.

Great Spirit guide my steps each day,
Knowing my heart to be true,
Help me to show others the way,
As I yield myself to you.

Ellen J Gouldsbrough

1

INNER WHEEL
(I)

E ACH soul has within itself powers. The power of thought and of the spoken word, the power to do good and the power to do harm, but the most important power of all is the power of selfless love. If worked with to allow it its full potential, this love can empower you to do many things all beneficial to the whole.

When you find this love, nurture it, as you will have found the greatest gift of all, for it is pure. It cannot be used to cause harm.

If all that you do, all thoughts that you have, concerning Earth and all universal life forms, is done with gladness of heart and sent forth on the wings of love, then, the seeds of those thoughts and actions will find fertile ground in which to grow, no matter where the wind may take them. It is in the light of these loving and positive thoughts and actions, that darkness will once again be brought into balance with light throughout all of creation.

Where upon Earth do you find the most rich and fertile soil? It is found in forests, woodland and in all the wild places. No artificial fertilizer has been applied to the soil, it has not been ploughed, and it is just natural and uncultivated. The leaves of autumn fall to the ground protecting it from the harsh winter frosts. Layer upon layer of leaves rot on the ground protecting and returning their richness back to the soil from whence they originated. The carcasses and excrement of all creatures that dwell within the area give back the nutrient needed to sustain their natural habitat. All in natural balance and all moving within the wheel completing the circle.

Let your thoughts and actions be as the autumnal trees, falling back to the planet that gives you so much. For as she gives so must she receive. In receiving, Earth is enriched. With such nurturing not only do you yourself benefit in your own evolution but so does Earth and via her the rest of the universe.

A tree's roots are firmly encased within the earth, but not in one spot alone. They spread a great distance away from the tree, the depth and spread of the roots meaning that they feed from farther afield, so that the nourishment the tree needs is taken from a wide area. In this way no one 'spot is depleted yet the tree flourishes. It grows strong and tall as it extends its branches toward the sunlight. Now and again a small distance away from itself a new shoot will appear, this is a part of its cycle.

The tree continues to live its cycle by sheltering the soil beneath it from both heat and cold, and by providing a home and playground for squirrels, a sanctuary for insects and a nesting place for birds, who can also perch in the tree's high branches to send their song out upon the wind for those who care to listen to hear and to gain enjoyment from their music.

Be like this tree with spreading roots, taking what you need from a wide area, so as not to deplete the planet. Let your thoughts and actions be like the rich soil that enables you to grow strong and tall, so that others may find safety and shelter by your side.

You will benefit from this by evolving a little more into who you truly are and not into who you have allowed yourself to become. Others will gain also because, with your protection, they will find the strength to grow.

Like the bird in the tree's high branches, your soul will also send its song out onto the wind, as it celebrates its new freedom. Its song will echo across the energies of the universe, so that all will know that a soul has found itself and is working for the good of the whole. Also that a flower is opening and turning its bloom to face the sunlight of pure love, to bask in and work with that light that is within us all.

When working this way you can rest assured that you are doing the will of the Great Spirit. You are benefiting the whole and doing your share of the housework.

As the suns, moons, stars and planets of the universe are kept in balance, so should you hold yourself. You have a mind, a body and a soul. These three must be kept in balance with each other. By letting your heart be the doorway for the energies to flow unimpeded between the three, you allow your mind to become a bridge between the higher and lower selves. The energies of the higher self along with its intuitions can be channeled through to the lower self and vice versa.

As you become more aware of your intuition, then you become more aware of your higher self. Actions then based upon this newfound intuition bring together the higher and lower selves. These actions, if done in love, will then have been done in a balanced way. You will therefore have sent out a stream of balanced energy into the ether to find its way to its resting point. If balanced and positive, then only good can come of it. If truly you have listened to your own intuitiveness, then no negativity should have been emitted.

Every soul has the same goal. To evolve and reach for the light. But just as planets revolve around each other in different orbits, souls intermingle on different pathways. Occasionally these paths may merge for a time, giving whomsoever is on them companionship and someone to help as they bring their experiences to this point. You will be able to give your companions the benefit of your experience, which may help them when it is time to move onward.

In this giving and receiving, both you and they will learn and grow. Do not, however, (except in special circumstances i.e. for a child's welfare) try and force your opinions upon others. Should this occur then neither you nor anyone else prospers. You may, in trying to force your ideas onto someone else, stop that someone from gaining the full value of what you are attempting to impart.

A seed that is gently sown, will find its own depth and will flower in its proper season. A seed that is sown by ramming it deeply into the soil, will not be such a full flower as it will have spent much of its energy pushing its way upward. By the time it reaches the light its time to flower will be at least partly, if not completely, over. In the same way by gently sowing ideas into people's minds, and letting them grow in their own time, a beautiful result will bloom. You may never see the result of the seeds that you sow in this way, but this is not really of any consequence. If they were sown well, then they will bloom at the correct time and in their own time will seed anew. Good thoughts and ideas sent out through the doorway of the heart, are the gentle seeds of creativity that will find their correct depth in the ever-shifting rhythm of the ether. Each will bloom in its own season.

Of course there are the seeds that have been forced out into the ether in the name of arrogance, ego and the "I know best syndrome". These seeds will be unable to find their correct depth and their flowers will try and choke the young delicate blooms that bring joy to whoever sees them.

For this reason, all thoughts and actions need to be done in a balanced way, with love and genuine concern for all life throughout the universe. Things done for the sole purpose of personal gain will achieve nothing beneficial to the whole.

To begin to seek your Inner Light, the light of love for yourself and for those known or unknown to you, you will need to be free of ego and be able to recognise the false picture of yourself, that you have been hiding behind. Until you can acknowledge and love who you truly are, you will never know your true beauty nor realise your true potential.

To dive into the fire and destroy the illusions that you have built around yourself, and to discard what you wish that you were, takes a great deal of courage. To admit to yourself and then to others that this is what you have done takes even more. But it is this type of courage that you will need for your own personal cleansing programme that will reveal your true self.

When popular opinion is against you, do you act as a sheep and follow because it is easier? Or do you stop and take time to consider what it is that you are trying to do, and for what purposes? If when you have contemplated and then decided that you wish to take action because your intuition says that you should, do you go ahead and do it? Or do you give way to opinion?

Your neighbour or friend is not you, and does not have the insight to know why you wish to take a specific action. Your path is your own individual one, chosen for you, because it is the one that will be most beneficial to you and those around you. If walked well, the repercussions will spread outwardly benefiting many.

Do not be a sheep. Be the dog among the sheep who helps the shepherd bring the flock home. There can never be enough sheepdogs for the flock is universal. The sheep may bleat and try to get away, but, the good sheepdog knows, that with patience and self-control, the sheep will eventually realise that it means them no harm and will then settle and allow themselves to be guided.

When you are true to yourself, you will be true to the whole, and will ensure that the light that burns eternally within your soul, can grow, enabling it to burn more brightly and purely. It cannot be doused for it burns from the very depth of your being. It will touch others and will be seen by all in existence who care to look. It will act as a magnet to those who wish their own light was brighter, and as a teaching aid for those who wish to learn.

Light puts darkness in its rightful place: it does not destroy it, as without darkness there would be no light. To have one the other must be, but balanced.

It matters not whether you have a university degree or left school at an early age, or whether you are rich or poor. None of these things affect the brightness of your light, for how brightly your light shines is dependent on what you have done, what you are doing and on who you truly are.

If your light has dimmed because of actions committed by you in the past, then do not worry unduly, for once you realise this you are in a position to make amends. Again courage is what will be called for. It is never too late to correct things done by you long ago that caused harm, as the reverberation of that deed will still be echoing across the universal energies. By now sending those energies good healing thoughts, the harm that was done can be repaired.

When you have completed your cleansing process and have tended the flame within and set it burning brightly, courage, faith and a belief that you can succeed will cause each action or thought done in love to add fuel to your flame, allowing it to burn brighter still.

Do not be afraid to ask for help. Neither you nor anyone is perfect. To ask for help will seek out others who, like yourself, are seeking a better awareness of themselves and of the role they have to play within the universe, to find out where their own individual piece of jigsaw fits into the whole puzzle. In this way you will give each other differing viewpoints according to your own qualities. For instance, one person may have the quality of patience and another the ability to think clearly. These two people can teach each other how to achieve these aspects in themselves. Through this giving and receiving, both will be able to develop at a greater rate.

It does not matter how many draw together in this way, each will have something to give and each will receive. It is not that one is superior to another, but just that each have their own qualities and experiences. Some will have experienced more than others and so will have more to give.

If you are in the happy position of being able to give more than you receive, do not feel cheated. You have found yourself in the right place at a time when others are needing help. To be able to give in such a way is reward in itself, as you will know that you have followed your path and that it is that path which brought you to this point. You will also take away with you the friendships of those you have helped, and this is also rewarding.

This of course must also be applied to the natural world around you, and to the planet that gives you all you need to sustain your life.

If you have found your light and are heaping fuel upon it that it may burn brighter, keep in mind that, as you quest, you will become more and more in contact with the natural world. When you accept this greater contact, the natural world may well ask something of you, perhaps when you are sitting in solitude.

If in one of these tranquil moments, a bird or wild animal, sensing the peace around you, comes close, do you congratulate yourself on your ability to create such peace and nothing more? Or do you think that the creature realises that you will not harm it and is here to show you its inner beauty as well as its physical beauty, and that it may have a lesson for you and has come to help you? Do you give thanks to the Great Spirit for enabling you to create a sense of peace about you and for guiding the creature to you, so that you may receive its lesson, and give it any help it may need in return?

There are many different ways that you can give this creature help.

Perhaps with a time of contemplation and meditation, you will discover how to use your skills and abilities to the best effect. With this meditation period you may see how to further the cycle of giving and receiving and so complete another stage in your development.

You will continue to learn in this way, for you will begin to take on a wider viewpoint, you will start to expand your mental faculties and begin to gain a better idea of the inter-action between life forms. This is an experience that you will then be able to relate to you own circle of friends, thus creating a wider circle of souls beginning to think with expanded minds.

CAN YOU?

Can you?,

Let the wind be your breath?

Let the sun be your heart?

Let the moon be your soul?

Let the rain be your tears?

Let the dawn be your smile?

Let the sunset be your frown?

Let the world be your love?

INNER WHEEL
(II)

W HAT changes would you like to see occur upon Earth? What do you perceive as being wrong? What do you think could be done to the conditions of the planet and all of her life forms?

If asked what you thought that you yourself could do to help bring about the necessary changes, what would your answer be? Would you reply?

       a) There is nothing that I can possibly do.

or

       b)   What's the point? It will never change.

Actually the answer is, that you can, in fact, do a great deal. Things can and will change if people allow their higher self its freedom and then follow its guidance.

Thought is solid. If you can envision the improvement that you would like to see, then you can do something to achieve it. It may be that one of the things that you would like to see is for the food being hoarded into giant mountains, to find its way to those that hunger. But can you do anything else along with approaching you local M.P, which seems to have few results in itself. Yes! You can visualise the food mountains being reduced as the food goes to the hungry. You can visualise the time when the well-fed members of the world will feed the undernourished ones.

As you visualise, send your visions out into the ether, onto the universal energies with clarity. Try not to jumble your thoughts, as, if you do, they will go out jumbled and will not have the desired effect. Do not rush, choose a time and a place where you can feel comfortable, relaxed and where you will not be disturbed, clarify your visions, order them, then with yourself in balance send them out. If time is taken to clarify exactly what you are seeking to do and as long as it is done with love and care for others, then your vision will join others of the same ilk and grow in strength, standing a better chance of coming to full fruition. As you send out your thoughts, wrap them in love and light so that they will be protected. If this is done with confidence, knowing that eventually good will come, then you will walk with a lighter step, for you will have given of yourself and will have been at one with the moment of the sending. You will know with certainty that you are able to help, and in sending such thoughts will have joined hands and hearts with so many around planet and with those who have already left her.

For thoughts and visions, such as these, to be successful, you will need to have faith in yourself, and in your capability, as well as in the outcome. In many tasks undertaken by you, even those of a material nature, faith in yourself has been required, so to have it for your vision of the future is really no different.

If whatever vision is sent, either large or small, is with the benefit of the whole in mind, you can be sure that the return will be bountiful. Deeds done with compassion and with no thought of self-gain, not only help others but also help to fan your flame so that it burns brighter.

By finding your light and working with it in this way, you free yourself from physical confines. In coping with the many difficulties that come your way, when beginning to work with the planet and the universal energies. You will be allowing your higher self the release to do what it knows should be done to help fellow family members, also for you to walk your path. But while your lower self refuses to acknowledge your higher self, it can do nothing but acquiesce.

Should you be foolish enough to use the power (for that is what it is) purely with self gain in mind, then although you will still receive a return, it will not be in the way that you planned.

You have free will. How do you use it? Do you use it solely for your own benefit, uncaring of the effect this has upon others? If so recall to mind the lesson of the sand. If you remain static then you force others to remain so. What right do you have to disallow another movement, or to cause them greater difficulty as they try to walk their paths? What cannot be accomplished by your ineptitude?

Or knowing that you have free will, do you seek guidance on the correct use of it? The less you exert free will then the more you give it up. The more it is given up, then the more free you become to work with your higher self for universal well being. To begin to use your free will less and less is very hard indeed, but you will be helped by those who are more knowledgeable than you, and whose vibrations are higher than yours, and whose task it is to guide you. If you free yourself, then you allow others the space to do the same. The more souls that free themselves, the more benefit it is for the planet, as they will become more attuned to Earth and will begin to see more, think more, and strive to work in a more positive way to heal her. This healing will result in Earth becoming more free, which will mean that the planets linked with her in the mesh, will also begin to free themselves and will raise their vibrations to accommodate Earth. So not only do you benefit, but so does Earth and also the universe.

Freedom is hard won. But it is within your capability. The flight of a free spirit is a wondrous thing to behold, as it signifies achievement. It means that confrontation has taken place. The tide of opposition, preconceived ideas, closed mind and tunnel vision, have all been at war with the light of truth within. Contemplation has taken place, intuition listened to, and the battle fought, with inner truth the victor. All who have the courage and the insight to touch their lights and fan them brighter will have begun to grease the axle on which the hub rests. The first steps to the good working order of the wheel.

If you have reached this state, what else can you do with your higher self now free to work with and teach your lower self? The answer being that you can achieve all that at this moment you are capable of.

Because all have differing capabilities, all have different goals to achieve. But no goal set is beyond each individual's potential. You may find that, in the process of fulfilling your goal, you experience degrees of difficulty. These difficulties help you to progress, and ensure that, when you finish your present task, you have gained in experience, and are fully prepared for the next.

Try to set aside each day a time when you can relax and receive healing. If you have crystals, then spend time with them, asking that they draw healing energy from the surrounding ether and pass it to you. If you do not have crystals, but are drawn to them, why not visit a place that sells them and see if there are any there for you? If neither of the above apply to you, then simply by uplifting your palms and asking for healing, you will receive it through your hands.

At the end of each stage of development, it is essential, to take time to relax, to be able to assimilate all that you have experienced and learned. To try and move forward without first doing this, would be folly. It would only increase the pressure on you, causing unnecessary harm. You also have, which makes demands on you, a physical life to lead. This must be balanced with your spiritual one.

In relaxation comes the release of the tension, which enables previously blocked energy to flow freely. To try to send healing and help out, without first letting go of tension, is to defeat yourself before you begin. Nothing can be sent out properly, if at all, from such tension. Also if you feel you are not achieving your aim, you will become more tense and more negative. This results in the wastage of time and of energy. So remember that before you begin, relax both mind and body. This is important and will enable the work you do, to be more beneficial.

When you have established a routine of relaxation, you will discover that you do not deplete yourself as much. This allows more energy to be available when working with your light. When you are accustomed to working in this way, and truly acknowledge your light, you will quite often discover, that by heeding more readily your intuition, your light begins to work with you.

If you are the type of person who finds it difficult to relax, or sit more than a few moments, think about going for a walk in woodland, or another totally natural environment. As you walk, breathe deeply and let your tension go. The trees and creatures of the area will then be able to give you the healing you require. For as you breathe you will be inhaling the harmonious and relaxing energy of nature. When you feel at peace, give thanks and ask that the negativity that you have released be turned to positive energy and returned to the surrounding area. This will complete the cycle and should always be done after any release. Negativity is no more use to the planet than it is to you.

The release of your tension is also beneficial to others, as once done, you will feel better and lighter in yourself. This you will pass on, in your smile, wave, joviality and so on to others, which will help them if they are not feeling good. Keep in mind that you are equally capable of passing on your dourness, as you are your happiness. It is always worth remembering that each has its opposite in all cases. There will be times, when experiencing severe difficulty and confusion, that you may be sorely tempted to give up what you are doing entirely. At these times, when faith in yourself and in what you are doing is being tested, go within and with wisdom so far gained, regain your clarity of purpose. It is a time when self-honesty is paramount. Ask yourself if the confusion and difficulty that you have been experiencing has occurred as part of a higher plan for you or whether it is self created. For instance does the reason for the work you are doing hold a greater percentage of selflessness or selfishness? If the latter is true, the answer is obvious. If the former is true, have you ignored repeatedly your intuition that has been telling you that something is not quite right? If so, then you will have been being guided to another section of your path. This may have been for a number of reasons. It may be that you have had company for a while, and the time has now come for you to separate and walk alone, to see what has been truly learned from your experiences and what not. Also how the lesson is applied in the future. To have ignored this will have created your harrowing experience.

Seeking the reason for your difficulty is not always easy and may need a great deal of time spent upon it. This is especially where a great deal has happened in a relatively short space of time. But when you are able to discover the reason for the confusion, then you dispel it. You will then be in the position to change course if necessary to once again take up your chosen path.

There will be times, when, no matter how you examine the situation, you can find no reason for the severity of the difficulty and will be certain that you are doing the right things. All you can do in these circumstances is continue on your way having faith that this is a part of the higher plan for you. At other times, you may be able to gain a vague idea of why you have had to endure confusion, but, if only vague, then keep it in mind and look again at a later date. It may well be that this is not quite the right time to discover the truth of the matter.

If you have a task to do that you feel yourself unable to do, and you are fighting against it, then until you are able to acknowledge that no matter how daunting it appears to you, it would not have been set if you were not capable of its fulfilment, and stop fighting, you will be unable to move on. This will have caused you mayhem and confusion. Ask yourself why you feel incapable. It may be because of experience you have buried deeply. But the results of this are seen in your self-doubt. If buried very deeply, then it is possible that you may not consciously be able to uproot it. In this case, gather all courage and attempt the task in question. It may take an inner battle. But if the result is you discovering yourself to be capable, where you believed yourself incapable, then you will have uprooted a poisonous plant. You will also have gained a little more experience and wisdom to draw upon and with which to teach others.

A BLADE OF GRASS

One single little blade of grass,
How often has it felt you pass,
Bent and flattened by many feet,
Even in cracks along the street
Though you do not feel its pain,
Given time it will stand again,
Should the blade be worn away,
The roots are strong and there to stay,
Fed and nourished by sun and rain,
The blade of grass will grow again,
It sheds its seeds upon the ground,
Fertile ground by some is found.
Animals and birds it also feeds,
They take only according to their needs,
The birds in trees then joyfully sing,
Their thanks to the blade for its offering,
Are you then as this blade of grass?
Bent and flattened as people pass,
Will you still be just as sweet,
When greeted by folk along the street,
When they try to wear you down
Will you smile or wear a frown?
Given no chance will you stand upright?
And strive to grow and serve the light?
Are you prepared to fight and battle?
To free yourself from chains that rattle?
So then you may truly start to grow,
A blade of grass your seeds to sow,
Many blades a meadow make,
Begin to grow for our planets sake!

Ellen J Gouldsbrough

2

THE MIDDLE WHEEL

The flame that you have found, and have been fanning, is sacred. It has come to you from the Great Spirit. Given to you at your creation. A gift to you so that you will always carry with you the guiding light that will lead you home when your journeying is over. If you fan it well, it will become a fire, which will light the way for many.

Fire itself has many attributes, both good and bad. The well-tended fire will create good things in abundance. It will receive fuel and oxygen in the correct proportions, and will be built within the safety of fire stones, with the tender keeping a careful watch over it lest it break free, and begin to consume the space around itself. Meanwhile it will be giving warmth and comfort.

Untended, it will have the opposite effect. Fuel and oxygen, in the wrong proportions, will either set it raging out of control, destroying anything in its path, (no one wants to be faced with a fire that has become a raging inferno emitting so much heat that none can draw near!) or, with not enough oxygen, will flicker and possibly die. If the latter occurs, then it has to be rekindled. Both these fires are not as efficient as the first.

Of the three types of fire, the one most warming and comforting, is the fire set within fire stones, fed the correct proportions of fuel and oxygen and kept an eye on. This is the fire of balance.

The one that is struggling through too much fuel and not enough oxygen, is a fire whose tender has become stuck in one way of working. Although he or she has good intentions, he/she has become tunnel visioned. This person walks their path but not fully. He/she does not look upward, nor from side to side, and see what other fruits and berries may be sampled. In the sampling of different fruits more oxygen may be allowed through to the fire, causing it to struggle less.

Across the planet, there are many different people from many different lands, whose heritage has been closely linked with the natural world for aeons of time. All have slightly different ways of working, and all have slightly different stories to tell, but all work for the whole family and do so in balance and harmony with the natural world. The tender of a well-balanced fire knows this and seeks to work with all.

The third fire, the raging inferno, emitting so much heat that it cannot be approached, is tended by the person who has gleaned as much information as he/she possibly could, from where-ever and whenever they could, but has not taken the time to put the fire stones in place. This person so badly wants to give, to share his/her knowledge and experience, that has become over zealous, pushing information onto any soul who looks as if they may listen. At times, not hearing the subtle, sometimes timid, questions asked of them. Missing the look of confusion on another's face, overlooking the fact that someone has taken a step backward to remove themselves from the fierceness of the heat. Not stopping to wonder if the recipient of the onslaught is ready to assimilate such knowledge.

This is how very good intentions can begin to destroy. You may have much more knowledge than another, but you need to be aware of the other person. You need to tread softly and to evaluate what another is able to comprehend at this time and what not. Always be the tender of a balanced fire. The flames may not leap to a great height, but they will burn for eternity if kept fed in the correct way.

Fire is light and light keeps darkness at bay. You do not need guns, bombs or nuclear weapons. Your are all members of one family, all living in one house. When bombs are dropped or weapons tested, the effects are felt deep within the planet itself as well as upon the surface. Residue from the explosion finds itself upon the winds being carried hither and thither. Nuclear waste is buried at sea or within the planet where, in many, many years to come, it will work its way into the soil and the sea-bed, causing untold harm to the natural world. Eventually it will find its way into the food chain, so becoming a weapon of destruction in many more ways than one.

You each have your weapon. It is the power of your thought, your speech, and your connectiveness to the whole. It is a weapon that can be used for the destruction of greed, the destruction of selfishness and the destruction of negativity. This is a weapon truly to bring about good that will not in any way subjugate another soul; no matter what form that soul takes. It is a weapon of freedom, to be used with deep insight as to the result of the wielding. It is also a weapon of healing, to be used in many different ways. Each time you wield your weapon of love and light, you will weaken the darker side of yourself and put it in its place. You will also weaken the effects that the darker side of souls have had upon the planet and your fellow beings - therefore weakening the effects of darkness throughout the universe. Any residue of power left by the use of this weapon, in the correct manner and frame of mind, can only be beneficial to planet. You can, if you begin to listen to your senses, tune in to the natural world and discover how to use your weapon and where to send your healing to the best advantage: another different way to complete the giving and receiving cycle.

Each time your weapon is used in this way, with much thought and awareness preceding it, not only does it become stronger but your fire becomes brighter and sheds more light, Earth will also be able to raise herself a little more and so can the universe. We all have the power to do something about the condition that we find our planet in. Some have more power than others at this moment in time, but do not leave it all to them. A tiny candle is able to light up a space that a larger one cannot get to. Many tiny flames can burn just as brightly - if not brighter - than a large one. If you leave it all to the ones whose flames are brighter, are you not becoming guilty of leaving your own fire untended allowing the possibility of having to rekindle it?

A tiny flame is as equally important as a large one. At this moment on the planet there are many more tiny flames than there are large ones. The large ones are able to help the tiny ones grow larger. You see, you cannot really opt out of your share of the housework. You can blame no one else for your lack of participation, you must accept this is your responsibility, for you are a part of the whole.

You have a nuclear family and an extended one. Think about your extended family. How far does it truly extend? Whose drops of blood run in your veins? Who were their extended family members and where did they come from? With this type of expanded thinking, perhaps you can begin to see how the family of mankind is one.

Do the same with your pets and houseplants, all of which belong to families. If you are able to love and care for a dog, a cat, bird and so on, can you not share the same feeling for their wild cousins?

Many of us co-exist with animals, birds, fish or plants. If we are able to do this in our homes, then to coexist and care for our wild places and planet as a whole should not be difficult. If you are able to care for your pets and plants when they are sick, then you are able to do the same for their relatives. It is to be hoped that your children are taught to respect and care for their pets, that they are taught to help their brothers and sisters, and taught not to tear leaves from houseplants. Can they not then also be taught the same lessons in regard to those life forms that exist beyond the front door? If it is wrong to pull leaves from houseplants, why it is not equally wrong to damage a tree? If it is wrong to neglect family pets, why is it not wrong to ill-treat their wild cousins?

Have faith in the natural world it will not desert you of its own accord for it gives you all you need. The trees give the oxygen that you breath; the willow, the raw aspirin for your pain; foxgloves give digitalis which is used for the treatment of the heart; the list is endless, as well as providing the food that you eat. In fact the planet, and all that lives and grows upon her, provides everything for your physical well being. Earth gives and continues to give. To complete the cycle you should be giving back if you are not already doing so.

When this type of thought process becomes the norm for you, and you begin to understand why you should, and how you can, return Earth's bounties, then you will be beginning to fulfil your responsibilities to the natural world, and to the whole. You will be able to discover more ways of fulfilling your responsibilities and by doing this you will begin to take your place properly within the universal family as well as beginning to lose your tunnel vision. This will result in another step forward for you, as well as for Earth. Your light will be a little brighter still from the usage of your weapon, and hopefully a seed will be sown that will encourage still further contemplation. Expanded thinking is able to place many different pieces of the puzzle into their correct positions, which allows more scope for further exploration.

In the act of becoming more aware of the whole, you will, in many cases, be discarding the ideas and teachings that you have grown up with. This will take a great deal of courage, as it is these ideas and teachings that have been the foundation stones upon which you have lived your life.

To now change your way of thinking, change your perspective and alter those foundation stones is going to be a challenge. Like all worthwhile challenges, it will call upon every ounce of courage that you possess. Look upon this as needing a new item of clothing.

You have far outgrown your old garment: you have worn it until the sleeves are too short, and it really does not fit around the waist anymore. You have had so much wear from it that it is now threadbare, and is much darned because you could not bear to be parted from it. Have the courage to let go of the old and don the new. You may be surprised at how well it fits and how the colour suits you.

If you intend to meet the challenge of a changing thought process, then do it for the right reasons, not because someone has told you to. Do it because, you have been given knowledge and have contemplated deeply upon it, and have reached the conclusion that it is the right thing to do. When done in this way, with much thought, you will be able to answer well any questioning, regarding your action, directed at you, from anywhere.

If, upon contemplation, you decide that you do not feel at ease with this, do not worry and contemplate again at a later date. It only means that it is a little too early for you to cope with a complete change of clothing. Should you try and force yourself before you are ready, then you will find that the garment does not quite fit, and the colour not quite right for you.

When your time comes for you to be rid of that comfortable piece of attire and for you to don the new, when you discover that you have successfully defended your action from the tide of opposition and persuasion that will come your way, you may find that you have had more success than you originally set out to accomplish, and where you least expected it to manifest. You may have set another thinking, even one whom you would have expected to remain in staunch opposition.

Having come through the stormy waters of change, the rain-clouds of self examination and the darkness of confusion all of which you will have experienced to reach this point Natural Law states that the waters must calm and the sun shine once again. This will bring the colours of the rainbow to any raindrop still lingering about you. With the coming of the sun and the stormy water safely negotiated, now comes the time for relaxation, whilst you settle in, as it were, to your new way of thinking and of doing things, and so be more aware of the huge picture that you are a part of. At this point, allow yourself time to drift upon the calm water, and to feel the ebb and flow of the energy around you, knowing that you are safe within the mesh.

You will have experienced change in the same way as a snake, when grown too large for its skin and has to shed it. This, in effect, is what you will have done at this stage. To relax now is essential, not only for your own well being, but also for that of the whole. Trying to rush into something new straight away could bring back the dark sky of confusion. Let the sun warm and dry your new skin before you venture forth once more. Assimilate all that you have learned. Place experience with learning. Which experience taught you which lesson? Why did such and such a thing occur in the way that it did, and what did you learn from it? In doing this you remove clutter and prepare the space for the next set of lessons. In the analysis of how you were taught, you will learn how to teach others, and how a lesson can be applied to the benefit of all that you are a part of. There may well be lessons that, as yet, cannot be taught, but will be when the time is right. You will just need to mentally file them away for future reference.

By this stage of your evolution your, light should be burning brightly indeed. You should have mentally transcended the confines of your physicality, with your higher self flying upon the thermals of universal energy. You should be on the brink of discovering what, apart from awakening yourself, you have been working towards. You will have been tried and tested and will have proved yourself capable of undertaking your universal tasks.

Whether those tasks are large or small, they will be the ones best suited to you. Just as with large and small flames, there are some who are best suited to the larger tasks, and many, many more best suited to the equally important smaller ones. Many souls working together, each at their own individual tasks can accomplish a great deal. Also, if the smaller ones are not done, then the larger ones cannot be done in a way that will gain most benefit for all life forms, as the larger will need to build upon the smaller.

You should now be able to gather together all that you have so far, and apply it in such a way that will help you think universally instead of just planetary. This, as well as slowly gaining the ability to see where events will lead both yourself and the Earth, will enable you to see the opposite side of the coin more easily. You will gain a newer, fresher insight into the whole, and find some understanding in the chaos around you. You will be able to have your feet firmly placed upon the planet, with your awareness being able to dance in the many different directions of the universe.

This does not mean that you will need the learnedness of a physicist if you are in fact, for example, a dustman. It means that as you walk your path physically, your higher self will be connected to the higher, purer vibrations and colours of the whole, and sending this awareness via your mind to your lower self. There will be the discovery that you are as aware now of the fact that there are other planets and life forms, equally if not more intelligent than humankind, as you were of your own small corner of Earth and your circle of friends. With this heightened awareness, whatever you do will be done with the overall good firmly in mind.

This is more responsibility for you and takes more courage, but with deep thinking, love in your heart, and by listening to the guidance of those whose task it is to guide you, then only good can come. At this stage you will have completed one circle, and now be fully prepared to begin another.

You should experience a sense of well-being as you realise that you truly do have the ability to help bring about changes for the better, which will hopefully be a better, more fulfilling, feeling than you had when you began.

Your own energy will be able to flow and mingle with the energies of the universe at higher vibrations. You will have found your present position in the network of the whole. Giving of yourself what is needed, your light will now be strong enough to work in this way, blending in as it were with the energies. Your thoughts and actions will be more powerful, as you will be able to draw the energies more easily into yourself, sending them back out to where you wish them to go.

Always remember to complete the cycle of giving and receiving, no matter how far you travel along your evolutionary path. Keep in mind also, that as you needed help in the beginning, others will also. Do not assume any kind of superiority, and bear in mind that you are always capable of learning more. There will be times when your lesson will come from one who is just beginning his/her own journey. Do not forget that the oldest, largest, tallest tree always returns to its source for nourishment, its roots still very firmly entrenched in the earth.

It is by always remembering where your roots lie that your tree is able to grow tall and strong, its branches reaching higher and higher, spreading wider, and wider. In this way you are able, when healing, to work upon the whole, being able to draw from universal energy that until now you have been unable to do. This power can be directed to the planet upon which you reside, as well as being drawn from the planet and sent to other parts of the universe.

Imagine yourself as a two-way power conductor, with energy passing backwards and forwards through you, running from source back to source, so completing a full circle.

To be able to be this type of conductor, you must at all times truly be aware of the whole, so that you can draw from all and return to all. You will need to work, at all times, with love, gentleness, awareness and wisdom, to keep in mind that all life forms come from, and will eventually return to, the Great Spirit. That the Great Spirit is the energy that creates the universal mesh, and has decreed your position and tasks within it. It is the energy and power that is used to help all forms of life. It is the sun that warms the day, the moon that governs the waters, the stars that guide our way. This self-same Great Spirit is both male and female in perfect balance, a quality that can be found in the tiniest insect to the largest mountain. Remember that all life is sacred: the ant is as important to the Great Spirit as the largest creature created, the least intelligent life form just as important as the most intelligent. All have the ability to teach as well as to learn. This is how true evolution of the soul is attained by the learning process and the application of the lesson learned.

You must remain aware, that all life forms vibrate at different levels. For example, crystals vibrate at a far higher and purer level than humans, who in turn, vibrate at a different level to plants. As was mentioned earlier in this book, it is all vibrational levels that go to form the whole. It would be advisable, perhaps, when sending healing to different forms of life, that you ask that the power be adjusted for that particular recipient. It is something that is done, but will help you remain aware of the different needs of the many different forms of life.

Colours also have vibrations. When you next look at a rainbow, think not only of admiring its colours, but also about the different vibrations that have created the colours and how well they merge together. This is also proof that differing vibrations coming together in the right way can create something beautiful. Consider the wonderful colours in a peacock's tail. In fact, the tail is colourless. It is in the different formations of the tiny hairs that form the feather, that when catching the light forms this spectacle. You also create your own colours that can be seen in the aura that surrounds you. If they are dim and dingy, it could be that you are not doing all that you could. The brighter and purer they are, then the more good you have been doing and the more you are able to do.

Once the point of being able to work with the whole is reached, and you are aware of the fact that there is a more refined power, and purer colours, that you are able to work with, it is time once more for you to look to that fire that burns within. To go once more, deep within yourself, with more knowledge, to seek the more elusive answers, quite probably answers to questions that you cannot actually form in your mind. Elusive answers to elusive questions! Questions that your higher self is asking. Take with you when you go within, the strength and wisdom of Mother Earth and draw from the highest vibrational level available to you at this time.

It is this constant seeking, questioning, and contemplating that will enable you to shed yet another skin, and to create the flames of your fire with higher vibrational colours. The very pale mauves, blues and white, and so on. Remember, that before white heat manifests itself, it will have first have had to travel through many temperature changes.

Never lose sight of the fact that no matter how far along your path you succeed in walking, you have been and still are helping to create sturdy spokes, that will stem from a strong hub, which should rest upon a greased axle. At this stage of your evolution, you will need to have the pliability that will enable you to change with the wind if it becomes necessary. We are in the process of mending the universal wheel. When a soul reaches this level of evolution, it can become quite possible that he or she may be asked to step in where another has not quite managed to do as well as was expected. If this happens to you, and you know the soul in question, do not castigate them, but help them, by explaining if you can, where they could perhaps have succeeded, or done a little better. Be as gentle as you can when this is done. Do not hurt another's feelings unnecessarily. Do not use harshness where gentleness should be. You do not know whether or not another soul once had to step in and help or even re-do a task that you had not done as well as it was thought you would.

It is not your place to judge. It is your place to play your part in the repairing of the wheel. It is in sharing stories of your own difficulties that you can help others overcome theirs. Do not tell only of your successes. This may make another feel inadequate. Wisdom comes when you can relate with as much relish your failures as well as your successes. This may show others obstacles that they may then be able to avoid and how to do it. Also, if others know that you have had your own failures, they will feel more able to approach you either with their own or for help when they find themselves in difficulty.

SOUL SONG

Soft springtime stars reflect in your eyes,
Warm summer winds caress in your sighs,
Pure autumn rains fall in your tears,
Sweet winter birds sing in your ears,
The rhythm of Earth envelopes your heart,
And completes the song of which your soul is a part.

3

THE OUTER WHEEL
(I)

TO have a sound rim, we must first have clarity of purpose. We must know, without a shadow of a doubt, that what we are all aiming for is the mending of the universal wheel once and for all. Repaired so well that the universe never again finds itself in such a position. When you can discover within yourself the determination to give, and to do, all that is within your power to ensure that no life form ever again suffers in the way they have and still are at this time suffering; then, along with other souls, who have the same determination, we have the firm foundation on which to build, and achieve the universal goal.

It is not enough to pay lip service alone, not enough to complete one or two tasks, and then decide that you have done enough and will now carry on with your own life. You need to give yourself fully to the Great Spirit, to be used in whatever way is necessary, to be of benefit to the whole. Once, after much thought, (for it should not be done lightly) you decide to give yourself totally, then you will be giving all that you are able, for yourself is all that truly belongs to you.

Any talent or gift that you have has been bestowed upon you by the Great Spirit. How can you use these to bring benefit to all? With meditation and contemplation, you may ask the question and receive the answer. When one task reaches its completion, why not ask, "What more may I do to help?"

By allowing the Great Spirit to come to you this way, and allowing the use of your gifts and talents for the overall good, then you can be certain that they are being used fully, and in a balanced manner to suit each occasion. It will also mean that all the colours of creativity will be brought into use at the correct levels for the particular task in hand.

If you are able to make this commitment, then you will feel more at ease with yourself, as deep down you will know that you are moving with the flows of spiritual energy, whilst also being a good power conductor. You of course will benefit personally, by allowing yourself every opportunity to evolve still further. Souls not attempting to evolve in any way will gain nothing. They will in effect be consigning themselves to stand in the darkness and watch as others dance with the myriad of colours that they have given themselves up to. You are responsible for your own evolution. Others can create for you the opportunity to evolve further, but cannot do it for you.

If you decide to make the ultimate commitment of giving yourself to the whole, then you will know that you have never truly left home. That Planet Earth is a part of your home that you are visiting for a while. In order that you can learn and to help restore her to her natural beautiful state where she can grow alongside of all her life forms. There will then be a celebration of all souls, whoever and wherever they are, who have been, and still are, working with the same commitment. All innocent life forms will join in with this celebration, as they will be able to form a union with those humans who are now walking with love for all uppermost in their hearts and minds. When this happy event is able to occur for you, then the energy of the natural world can merge with your own, forming a bond upon which you will be able to give more of yourself in the moment of giving, and to receive more in return. The universe will sing with happiness as another soul has woken and is showing the way to others. You will rejoice in the knowledge that you have once more joined fully with the energy that is around you.

The natural world does not have a mantle clock telling it when to wake, work, eat and sleep. Each bird, animal, fish and insect, flower and tree does all of these things according to their own individual natural clocks. When you are able, as much as is possible, to live by your own natural clock, then, not only will you feel a little better in yourself, but a little more in tune with the world around you.

Many are now able to see themselves as an extension of the natural world, they can see clearly that humankind is not superior as a life form, but just another species. These are the beings that must bear responsibility for correcting all the wrong that they have done. They must repair all that they have broken, opening themselves to accept any new task that the Great Spirit asks of them. They will have rid themselves of any last vestiges of ego, and will be able to accept who and what they truly are.

There are many souls upon the Earth at this time whose task it is to help. They too have had much to learn, to enable them to teach and show others how to coexist, totally, with the planet they dwell upon, how to become more aware of the wholeness of the universe and the continuity of the life-force, within all that can never die. Souls need to realise that they are transient beings, passing through many lives and spheres of existence on their journey back to the creator, but always with the task to evolve, and to realise that no-one is an island no matter how much they feel they would like to be.

It is the responsibility of every man, woman and child, to begin to, and continue working for, the whole. A child can give as much proportionally as an adult. Therefore do not tell a child that it cannot help, or ignore it. Remember that the child has left the realm of spirit more recently than you have. Also keep in mind that the love of a child is unconditional. If treated properly and with respect, he/she will retain the unity with the whole that it had when born to the Earth. It is in the way when children are ignored, neglected, and taught to be overly materialistic, that they are taken out of balance, and can become more difficult than a little one has the right to be. A child needs to be taught but not beaten.

Children in many ways learn from the examples that they see around them. To be around parents and family who care about the rest of humanity and the world about them, will generally, (although there are always exceptions) grow up with the same caring attitude. On the other hand, those reared with the "As long as I'm alright, it doesn't matter about anyone else" attitude around them will generally grow with the same outlook. This latter doctrine is no more help to the child than to the adult. Just as the parent or adult has disallowed themselves true growth, they now deem it fitting to apply this to the child. This constitutes neglect. Not only do parents have the responsibility for the physical wellbeing of their children but also for the spiritual. A young child is without prejudice until taught by an adult. With so much negativity around, why do some adults see fit not only to condone such negativity in a child but also to teach it?

Children will continue to suffer, both at the hands of each other and adults, until the adults become honest enough to admit to themselves that they can be wrong, apologise to their child, and rethink their attitudes, thus re-teaching the child. In this way, the planet also will begin to benefit, as in this learning children will not have their basic, instinctive, respect for the natural world suffocated. To bully is to show weakness, whereas to be gentle shows great strength. As well as teaching, a child learns from it. When wonder is seen in a child's eyes, look with those eyes and let your own open in the same wonderment at the innocent beauty that the child has seen. Look, learn, and re-learn. Children are simple logical souls. It is the adult that creates the complicated child, by forcing issues that should not be forced and not forcing the issues that should. By not listening, or, if listening, not truly hearing what the child is trying to say.

Life in reality is simple though not easy. It is we who make it chaotic for ourselves, trying then to lay the blame at someone else's door rather that at our own.

The wellbeing of Earth and the universe is, at the moment, in the hands of every adult who together constitute the caretakers. The future wellbeing is in the hands of the present-day children. They must be shown and taught how to take on the mantle of responsibility that will one-day rest upon their shoulders. The present-day caretakers must ensure that the planet is back in her rightful state, so that the young have something to take responsibility for! The sins of the fathers are not for the children to atone for. The sins of the fathers ensure that all children suffer. Each must take responsibility for his/her own actions and atone for them if necessary. To give yourself once more to the Great Spirit will bring back the simplicity, the wonder, and the love for yourself and for all other forms of creation.

When all colours, creeds and ages can come together on one Earth, beneath one sky, with the same sun to warm us, the one moon to lighten the night sky, and the same stars to guide us, THEN will we truly begin to create a solid rim for the wheel of the universe.

The most beautiful soul may well be locked into a malformed or ugly physical shell. Those who would deny themselves the opportunity of learning about, or from, another just because their physical shell is not the correct colour or pleasing to the eye show themselves to be foolish. Discover your true eyes and look deeply into another's. The eyes mirror the soul within. As has been previously stated, all are capable of teaching as well as of learning. Souls who find themselves thrust together usually have a little of both to do. There are many different ways to reach the same destination. All are ways for all souls working towards one goal. Your way may not be right for another, although that does not mean that either is wrong as long as both are working to benefit the whole.

As well as opening your eyes, open your mind and your heart to what is occurring everywhere upon the planet. Ask yourself why? What could the planet herself be trying to make us hear? Look at each situation deeply. Do not look at the surface alone. The surface is the hard shell that needs to be broken for the kernel to be obtained. Examine the fruit of a situation, then taste it. Until it is tasted, you will not know whether it is bitter or sweet. Some fruits may be bitter if tasted before they are ripe, but sweet when they are. Sometimes you will be faced with a situation that displeases you, that perhaps you find bitter to the taste. If the situation is handled properly then when the kernel of the difficulty is reached it may well be sweet and palatable.

There may be times and circumstances when you feel that you are under attack or are about to be attacked for what you are tying to do. Try not to attack in return. Side step for a while until your assailant grows weary of constantly missing the target. Then speak gently and quietly and with love, asking why the other feels so threatened by you. Bring peace back into the situation, so that you are able to answer the allegations clearly, and be heard clearly. This positive, but not pompous, attitude will negate the negative one. If all souls who are already walking their paths can each do this, then slowly those who are taught in this manner will learn and will begin to teach others. They will be in a stronger position to do so, because they will have the full understanding of why souls feel threatened in particular circumstances, where many of us would be having to learn by having the reasoning explained to us. However, we must all try to understand the fears that many souls have, for until we do, we cannot help, as fully as we should, others to awaken and to take their first steps toward enlightenment and awareness. This in order that they, in their turn, will come to know that what they do, is done because it is the right thing to do. To know that listening to their own intuition and having faith has been the correct way after all and that they are walking their own paths towards home. That after the difficulties, the fruit has been reached and is indeed palatable. Also to know that though errors may well be made in the future, if they continue to walk the road of love and light, they will be living in peace and balance, therefore in harmony. When harmony amongst all life forms is regained upon Earth, then it will begin to be regained throughout the universe. Every soul ever created should be working towards this end. This is when souls will find it pleasing to be incarnated upon a planet rather than something to be endured.

The time spent preparing and awakening souls upon Earth who are sleeping, some more deeply than others, will be difficult. At times many will act as a bear who, on waking from his long winter slumber, discovers that he has slept over long and that breakfast is not quite as good or as plentiful as it should be. With patience and perseverance, you will discover that as these souls awaken, they will begin to do the same as you, and begin to find their true selves. Again, the fruit will be sweet to the taste buds, for the many souls doing this will help Mother Earth to raise her vibrations without suffering unnecessary pain and anguish.

Planet Earth is beautiful, with many more life forms upon her than on any other planet. She is the garden of the universe. In any well-tended garden, weeds must be kept to a minimum. There is the need to protect the flora and fauna of the planet. Many species, as all know, are becoming extinct. Why? Because humankind is greedy. That they want they take, heedless to the effects of their actions upon the natural world. It is not the natural world that has created the situation that results in Earth's vibrations being too low. The natural world lives in balance. It is the so-called "civilised" peoples of the world where imbalance is most prevalent. Think carefully. Is it the action of a "civilised" people to hoard food whilst others starve? Is it the action of a "civilised" people to deliberately cause another life form horrendous pain in the name of vanity? A fur coat is absolutely beautiful when worn by the animal that it belongs to.

The so-called "uncivilised" peoples of the world in fact prove themselves to be the more civilised. They live each moment in balance with, and a part of, nature.

They take only that which they need, not wasting anything and always giving in return. The nomadic peoples, just by being nomadic, never deplete any one area, as once they move on, the place that they evacuate is always able to regenerate itself.

There are many life forms not living upon Earth, who are both peaceable and caring souls, who have a great deal of knowledge to impart, but cannot at this time do so, for the attitude upon Earth at this time makes it dangerous for them to do so.

There are also those who are not peaceable and caring, who also have knowledge that they do not wish to impart, for theirs is knowledge that enables them to gain control. It is knowledge that they want to use for their own ulterior motives. The attitude of people on Earth at this moment is far more conducive to the latter extra-terrestrials than the former. It is time that we upon Earth raise our heads from the sand, open our eyes, and begin to make it more conducive and safe, for the former to draw closer so that they are able to help, instead of drawing, like a magnet, the latter. The responsibility lies very firmly at the feet of each soul upon Earth and those who are being born at this time. There are amongst them many special souls. Perhaps one may be among your family members already, or perhaps one is due to be born. For these souls to be able to do their jobs when they are grown, you must first do yours.

THE INVITATION

Come and spend some time with me,
Look and tell me what you see,
Spread your wings and fly with me,
Fly up high what do you see?
Am I truly as you thought?
A chunk of soil and good for nought?
Or a living, breathing form
Constantly battling an ongoing storm?
Truly alive or slowly dying?
Is that a two legs I now hear crying?
No! This surely cannot be,
At last they're beginning to care about me.

Ellen J Gouldsbrough

THE OUTER WHEEL

(II)

EVERY soul has the right to free flight. It is in flying freely on strong winds that we are able to draw from the whole and return to the whole in equal proportions. This may be done in whatever way we find best suits us, perhaps alone through meditation or contemplation. Maybe with a group of like-minded individuals who have committed themselves to the whole, who wish to fly and feel the warmth of the universal air currents flow through them. Maybe in moments of quietude whilst bathing or just before sleep, in the woods or near the sea.

The true release of your soul comes when every thought, word and action, even if, through necessity, harsh, is done in and through love. When, for the sake of others, you are able to act selflessly and sacrifice all that you are able to, you can fly freely with the strong wings of love for all. When you are able to see that all your heartaches and problems have not been visited upon you by the Great Spirit for any malicious reason: but with love for you, so that you could to learn, and in this way be helped. When you are able to understand that although we have the Great Spirit, it is our rite of passage and not the Great Spirit's. We cannot learn and appreciate the exhilaration of free flight if we sit upon our nest and expect another to fly for us.

"If there is a God, how can He let such terrible things happen?" is a cry most often heard from the souls who walk upon the planet. The answer is that it has not been the Great Spirit allowing it. Those who walk upon the planet are the ones who have allowed, and who continue to allow, these horrors to be. The Great Spirit cannot do it for us, just as a parent cannot sit in a classroom and learn for a child. The child must be present with the teacher to learn, as we must be with the Great Spirit to learn how to fly. Just as parents everywhere chastise their children, we must also expect harsh words, and smacked wrists in one form or another, when we persist in wrong-doing by endangering our home and our brothers and sisters of the universe. We are all children of the Great Spirit. The universe our classroom. If we heed our teachers well enough, then though the final examination may be difficult, we should have no fear of failing. With so many wings capable of strong flight and all working together, we will be able to lift our planet higher and allow her own form of free flight.

With this type of understanding and work, you will, as you progress further, find that more and more knowledge is available to you. Bringing with it an ever greater understanding of the wider picture, and providing you with more material for further exploration. Enabling you to work in many more ways than you had previously been able. Also bringing you into contact with others from around the world, who will be able to help you discover even more.

There are many souls who have a great deal of knowledge and understanding, and who are beginning to travel the world to impart their knowledge, so that from each single pebble the ripples are able to spread even further afield, touching more and more souls, who it is hoped will reciprocate in like manner. All who teach will teach the outlines and guidelines so that you are able to work to help all. They will give ideas and help, but the recipients must do the actual work themselves. Each teacher has, before he/she is able to teach, learned his/her own difficult lessons, and know that he/she is still learning. They know that it is quite possible for teachers to learn from their pupils, and are ready and eager to learn any lessons that pupils have to teach them. This will enable them to teach a little better and more fully.

Do not set yourself apart from them. They are doing the tasks appointed to them by the Great Spirit, and come in many shapes, sizes and colours. They are the seeds carefully sown by the Great Spirit. Do not assume that the colour of the physical shell necessarily denotes the colour of the soul within. At this time there are many souls who dwell in a shell the colour of which does not match their true colour. The souls within these shells are in that particular shell and country because of the job that they have to do, so that in this lifetime they receive their final training for their chosen task. They will also have experienced many different lifestyles since their creation, finally coming to rest in the part of the world where they are most needed. They dance their steps in the universal wheel and will continue to do so. This is an important time for the whole universe but particularly Earth and all of her life forms. Earth can wait no longer. She must cleanse herself to enable her to raise her vibrations. It would be beneficial both to ourselves and to planet if we were to help her accomplish this just as she has always helped us.

You are able to draw power and healing through yourselves to cleanse and heal your own chakra system. The planet also has a chakra system. Each one channelling power through their own system to the planet will enable her to do much, as the power will be running along ley lines, which can be likened to a blood stream. Just as in humans, the blood carries nourishment to each cell of the body, so the ley lines do the same for the planet. The power running along the ley lines will be able to strengthen the weak spots and thus return to full working order many powerful points around the planet. With these lines fully repaired and operational, and carrying the full power-load that they should, then we should be able to slowly see a difference in the natural world around us. In the British Isles alone there are many stone circles. In England there are the Henges, the most famous of which is of course Stonehenge, which is the most powerful of its trinity at the moment, but what of Avebury Henge or Wood Henge? What are they and others like them, able to do when fully healed and fully powered? This is only one example, there are many more around the world. All on the planet bear the responsibility for healing and bringing them back into play once more, so that Earth is able to be as she should be. You do not have to travel to these places in person to give healing, for it can be done via absent healing.

This can be done because the Earth herself shows us that this is possible. In summers of intense heat, when the lush green grass of springtime is reduced to the brown of dryness and death, when all that is seen around us is the dark colour of the soil, when once again the rain returns to the soil, the grass once again begins to send up new green shoots. The leaves upon the shrubs and trees cease to fall, as the healing life-giving water, with all its minerals, nourishes the soil and once more gives new life to the flora of the planet.

Figuratively speaking, Earth herself is suffering from the lack of the life-giving waters of love. She is drying up and becoming dark soil alone, as she becomes desolate from the desecration that human kind inflicts upon her in so many different ways. By now re-learning, and entering whole-heartedly into the dance of creativity and love, our actions and thoughts will become the gentle rains full of nourishment that will fall upon the earth, reversing the desolation and allowing new life to spring forth once more.

Earth at this time, is gripped within the harsh frosts of winter at the end of her present cycle. She has moved around the wheel full circle, and should now be able to begin her new one. Humans have created about her, huge ice packs that grip her tightly, refusing to allow her to move on. Winter should give way to spring: the time of renewal, when a new cycle begins: the sun higher in the sky should melt the ice, so that the rivers and streams flow freely. This is the time when the snows should disappear, revealing tender new shoots that have been kept warm by its blanket. The time when the birds should sing to us for longer periods as they prepare to bring forth new life. Just as humans have created for Earth the harshest of winters, that has gripped her in the densest of ice packs, we must now become the planets springtime. The warmth of our love must be as the sun that is higher in the sky, so that it melts the ice and snow, allowing the streams and rivers of universal healing to flow. Our actions, the gentle spring rain that nourishes the new shoots of creation. Our commitment, the blustery winds that blow away the dust and debris from others, so that they may join in and send the sun even higher in the sky. Eventually spring must give way to summer, which is when we see the full results of the spring, in the fruit and flowers, and in the young fledglings as they begin to take flight.

If only we who are winter will become a balanced spring, then we will enjoy the summer and the fruits of our labours as Earth's summer will be absolutely glorious, and her autumn bountiful. Therefore so will our own.

Souls will have broken down the barriers of fear, and lack of confidence, and will know that the Great Spirit loves and cares for each part of creation and so can they. As well as knowing that we have the love of the whole surrounding us, and working with us as well as through us. To begin, all must open themselves to feel for each other. Lies, deceit and generally avoiding the truth, all go a long way to ensure that we do not show our true selves, which helps us to hold Earth in winter. Many of life's experiences cause us to build barriers in our minds and walls around ourselves in order to try to protect ourselves from such pain being felt again. In doing this, though, we trap the pain within in, not overcoming it and then letting it go. This then begins to eat away at who we truly are and at our capabilities. We then either, unknowingly or knowingly, pass these negative feelings on, so creating more negativity. We become so bound up in keeping ourselves safe that we do not see where the bad experience has helped us, then being able to temper its effects upon us, so ensuring that it does not affect others. After all, it was our experience, so why should it have a detrimental effect upon some one else. Negativity seeps from us to our surroundings and from there to Mother Earth herself. When each and every one can become more positive than negative, then the sun will climb higher in the sky as the positive seeps through to heal the damage done by the negative. This is not an easy thing to do but can be accomplished.

To be uncaring and cruel enough to laugh at another's misfortune will invade their sacred space and cause them pain. Love and concern will also invade that same sacred space, the difference being that one will be gentle and healing, the other harsh and detrimental. This is also applicable to the planet. To be cruel and uncaring to life forms is a destructive force finding its way into the planet. To be caring and loving to all life forms is a positive force finding its way into the planet. Which one is the better?

It is negativity and selfishness that caused the wheel to begin to crack in the first place. There were too few awake and prepared to work to arrest it. They could not hope to arrest alone such a destructive onslaught. Now all must awake and join them. Together we can arrest the break and begin to repair it.

All must recognise within themselves, the negative as well as the positive aspects of their character. Once negativity is accepted and worked upon it can be turned to positive action. In this way the whole person is being nurtured instead of just a part.

As negativity is released and turned to positive energy, then Earth is also being helped, as the energy received by her will be healing instead of destructive. As you concentrate upon turning your weaknesses into strengths, you undergo metamorphosis, from, as it were, a caterpillar into a beautiful butterfly. You will not only have helped yourself, but will also have helped the rest of creation to metamorphosise, yet again indicating how closely inter-linked in the mesh of the whole we all are.

As you give so shall you receive. This may not materialise within your present physical lifetime. The rewards are waiting for you when you leave the physical after each Earth walk.

This is one way of ensuring that what is given is given selflessly. If it were any other way, then, once the discovery was made, too many souls would give purely to receive material gain. This would be of benefit to nothing nor to no one.

It may well appear that there are many upon the planet who always seem to get on well no matter what they do, who appear to have few worries and who apparently suffer far less hardship that others. If this is truly so, it is because their time for testing has not yet come. Many physical lives are long in duration, thus plenty of time for testing. The shorter the span the more compact must be the testing. For some whose final walk is in progress, testing of greater intensity is called for. They are ready to move further from Earth and begin a new cycle in their evolution. Therefore they are now having to prove that they have truly evolved and are in effect taking their diploma. These souls have much courage and are in themselves rays of pure love and light.

They have gone through, during their passage, much the same as everyone else. They are able to bring together the colours (in as pure a form as possible upon the Earth Plane) of universal healing energy. They are, on the whole, more instinctive, patient and gentle than those who are not as yet so evolved. It is towards these attributes that all should be working.

Love is light and light is love. If you know of a soul who has tried all but who appears to be in receipt of nothing, and who, though struggling constantly, will not turn away from love and light, someone whom you know that you can always rely on in times of need, no matter what has gone before, try to learn from them as they are most likely to be one of the highly evolved and, in most cases, old souls. These souls have much wisdom and compassion. They truly dance with the whole of creation. These souls are the teachers, who await your contact with them. They will not seek you out. They await you to seek them, as then you will be ready to learn that which they will teach. You may not easily find them but they are there among you. If they were easily sought out then many who were not yet ready, but who thought that they were, would find them too early, thus causing confusion in the seeker.

You cannot perform a dance until you first learn the steps. Once the steps are well learned, then, as soon as you hear the music, you will dance with unthinkingly true steps. The creator of this dance is the Great Spirit. We, his children, are in the process of learning how to dance it. We know what the dance is about, but many seem unable to comprehend that the most intricate steps are easily executed. If we busily stand telling ourselves that we do not have the agility to perform the steps, then we are not looking properly. We have not taken the time nor had the patience to simply break the steps down and look at the tiny individual movements that go to create the steps themselves. We are in fact looking at the surface alone and assuming that we must perform in one difficult movement the whole thing, instead of seeing how they are built up and performing them that way. If we learn thoroughly each tiny movement in the correct order, then no matter how complicated the overall dance is, we will perform it well and with ease.

If mending the universal wheel seems to you to be fraught with difficulties, then look more closely and deeply to see how the many smaller steps will eventually come together and, when performed, will be done with ease. Humankind appears to find it easy enough to dance the steps to the dance of destruction, but this is not the choreography of the Great Spirit. The dance choreographed by our Creator is the dance of creation and rebirth. You must forget the steps that have been danced by so many for so long, that bring about disharmony, imbalance and result in destruction. You must re-learn the lighter, more joyous steps of the Great Spirit.

There are many of the more highly evolved souls who are now qualified to teach the steps. These souls have learned how to dance with the whole. They hear the music to their own part of the dance and perform their steps with grace.

To mend the universal wheel is the purpose of the dance and must be the outcome. After that we do not know. We do not have that knowledge nor indeed the wisdom to be allowed it, though some may have their own vague ideas. Only the Great Spirit has this knowledge, but we can be certain that once the universe and all of creation is as it should be, there will be more. We will have learned and have been prepared to do whatever is expected of us in the future.

MY GIFT TO YOU

My bow is strong and my arrow true,
As a streak of light it flies to you,
To brighten up your darkest night,
Bringing love to ease your plight,
You do not know me but I am here,
Just like you I know much fear.

Many souls have passed by me,
Their eyes were closed so they did not see,
The light of love that reached out to them,
A full blown flower on a slender stem,
My friends are the birds, the flowers and trees,
My thoughts are sent on the gentle breeze.

I thank the Earth for her many gifts,
And hope to help her as she lifts.
I pray this book has helped in some way,
A gift of love to all on this day,
Remember me when I am gone,
I was a place where the sun once shone.

Ellen J Gouldsbrough